100 Must-Do

RIO DE JANEIRO

Travel Guide

Outdoor Adventures, TOP 5 Beaches in Rio (Copacabana), Historical and Cultural Sights, Eat Drink, Cool Cafes, NOT tourist places, Unusual Hotels and Hostels, Souvenirs!

Table of Contents

TO VISIT

Historical and cultural sights

Copacabana

An area of Rio that boasts one of the most famous beaches in the world, Copacabana has many areas of interest including a mosaic tiled promenade, crescent shaped beach, hiking trails, Arpoador, Fort Copacabana and architecture hailing to its glory days. Bairro Peixoto and Lido display their respective art-deco and art-nouveau architecture for visitors to marvel as they stroll down the streets. Although it is starting to show its age, Copacabana is still home to some great shopping and entertainment districts with cinemas and theatres.

Fort Copacabana

A seaside fort located on a small peninsula jutting into the Atlantic Ocean, Fort Copacabana provides spectacular views of the ocean and beaches. Originally opened as a military base in 1914 to protect the entrance to Guanabara Bay, the fort was closed in 1986. Since then it has become a museum featuring exhibits of the Brazilian army. The fort has many amenities which include two cafés and live concerts once a week. A recommended must do is to have brunch at the Fort. Open Tuesday-Sunday 10am-6pm.

- Avenida Atlantica, 4240 Posto 6, Copacabana, Rio de Janeiro, 22070-020

Cathedral of St. Sebastian

St. Sebastian is the Catholic patron saint of Rio and the Cathedral of St. Sebastian is the seat of Rio's arch diocese. Work began on the cathedral in 1964 and took 15 years to complete. The result is a monumental cathedral that is styled after the Mayan pyramids. At a height of 96 meters with a diameter at the base of 106 meters this cathedral towers over the landscape. Four stained glass windows each reaching 64 meters from the floor to the ceiling make this area which can seat up to 5,000 people bright and spacious. Open daily 8am-5pm.

- Avenida Rupublica do Chile 245, Rio de Janeiro, 20031-170

Leblon

A section of Rio that is split into two areas, Upper and Lower Leblon, it boasts some of the safest and most upscale residences of the city. The upper area, Alto Leblon, has high end restaurants, shopping and entertainment. The lower end, Baixo Leblon, has a more bohemian vibe that extends to the beach and the ocean. Leblon is also home to one of the most scenic drives in Rio, the Av. Niemeyer. A great place to walk around and take in the sights of a residential area.

Botafogo

An area of Rio that has a vibe reminiscent of Soho, Botafogo is known for its bistros, cinemas, malls and bars. Home to the Botafogo de Futebol e Regatas football team, this mostly upper middle-class area has safe, tree-lined streets. Here you will find the Indian museum, Rio Sul one of the largest malls in the city and lots of great bars and cafés. A short climb to the top of Morro Dona Marta will give you a panoramic view of the city.

Corcovado

The mountain in the heart of Rio that is home to the iconic Christ the Redeemer statue, Corcovado is a 710m peak of granite stone. Part of the Tijuca Forest, the peak's steep eastern face and gradual western face exemplify the forces of nature on the Rio coastline. Due to its elevation, Corcovado can be shrouded in clouds or mist from time to time. It is highly recommended that you wait until the morning of your trip up the mountain to purchase your tickets.

Santa Teresa

An area located in downtown Rio, Santa Teresa is known for its historic and artsy charm. Home to the Ruins Park and the Santa Teresa Tram, Museu da Chácara do Céu art museum, the Armazém São Thiago restaurant and the studios of many artists, it is not to be missed. You can get there by climbing the Selarón Stairway which joins Lapa and Santa Teresa. One event to attend in Santa Teresa is the Mercada das Pulgas a samba celebration. This celebration occurs on the first and third Saturday of each month and only costs R$10.

Fiscal Island

Located in Guanabara Bay, this small island is home to Brazil's customs agency which is housed in a building that looks more like a storybook palace than the home to a government agency. The Fiscal Island Palace was finished in 1889 under Emperor Pedro II and held the Brazilian Empire's last Imperial Ball before becoming a constitutional monarchy. The lime-green palace is now a museum with a naval focus. Admission to the museum is R$25. Tickets and transportation are available at the Naval Museum on the mainland.

- Avenida Alfredo Agach, s/n Centro, Rio de Janeiro, 20040-020

Christ the Redeemer

Perhaps the most recognized image of Rio, Christ the Redeemer statue towers on top of Corcovado Mountain. Standing at 38 meters high the art deco statue is heavily photographed. Made out of soapstone, it is one of the modern wonders of the world. Commissioned by the Catholic Church in the 1920s, sculpted in France and finally inaugurated ten years later, Christ the Redeemer is visible from anywhere in Rio. Admission is R$62 for adults and R$40 for children. Open Sunday-Saturday from 8am-7pm.

- Parque Nacional da Tijuca, Cosme Velho, Rio de Janeiro, 22241-330

Catete Palace

Built in the late 1860s Catete Palace is a grand home and former presidential palace located in the Flamengo neighbourhood. Today it is known as the Museu da República and is home to a museum, café, bookstore and theatre. Neoclassical in design, the palace displays paintings, sculptures, motifs and furniture from both Brazil and France. The gardens surrounding the palace feature ponds, grottoes, trees and a playground. The entrance to the palace is R$6 while the gardens are free. Open Tuesday-Friday at 10am-5pm and Saturday-Sunday at 11am-6pm.

- Rua do Catete 153, Metro Catete, Rio de Janeiro, 22220-000

Sao Bento Monastery

Still a viable monastery today, St Benedict's was originally founded in 1590 and finished being built 80 years later. Comprised of the monastery and Our Lady of Montserrat, Sao Bento overlooks the Guanabara Bay. Our Lady of Montserrat has a humble exterior which gives way to a rich, baroque interior. Elaborate carvings and paintings compliment the chandeliers which illuminate gold filigree that covers many surfaces. Public Mass is held daily with Gregorian chants included on Sunday mornings during High Mass. The monastery itself is open at specific times and only permits men to enter.

- Rua Dom Gerardo 40, Centro, Rio de Janeiro, 20090-030

Candelária Church

The Igreja de Nossa Senhora da Candelária, is Rio's oldest and most culturally significant churches. Dating back to its founding in 1630, the church as seen today opened in 1898. A mix of baroque and neoclassical styles, the façade is fairly demure while the interior is full of colour, texture and light from the marble columns to the stained-glass windows to the rich, colourful paintings adorning the walls and ceilings. Mass is held daily.

- Praca Pio X, Rio de Janeiro, 20040-020

Museum of Tomorrow

The internationally recognized Museu do Amanhã opened in late 2015. It is a contemporary designed building that houses a museum for sustainability. In addition to its unique exhibits that contemplate human impact on the environment and social issues, the museum is also known for its architectural design. Spanish architect, Santiago Calatrava designed the building with a large, futuristic entryway. Located in the port district which has been undergoing a regeneration over the past decade. Exhibits are in Portuguese, Spanish and English with admission costing R$20. Open Tuesday-Sunday at 10am-5pm.

- Praca Maua 1, Rio de Janeiro, 20081-240

Maracanã Stadium

Originally opened for the 1950 FIFA World Cup, the Marcanã Stadium is the largest stadium in Brazil. When it opened it had a capacity of 200,000 but has been reduced after several renovations to less than 80,000. Controversy surrounded the site following the 2016 Olympics when it fell into disrepair and was damaged by looters. New management has since taken over and re-opened the venue. It is home to the Brazilian National Football Team, CR Flamengo and Fluminense FC as well as a site for large concerts. Admission to games is R$40-80 and the sports museum is R$20. Open daily at 9am-5pm.

- Av. Pres. Castelo Branco, Portao 3, Rio de Janeiro, 20271-130

Lapa

Lapa is the night district of Rio and home to the Arches, the Roman-style aqueduct. The Archers is a popular venue for street parties that last into the early hours with food and drink sold by vendors on the street. A place to visit to see the cultural night life of Rio, during the day, you can walk around to see some of the street art which is most prevalent around the Selarón Stairway. Streets are closed to vehicles on Fridays, Saturdays and Sundays which allows for a festive vibe.

TO TASTE

The Most Delicious Things to Eat & Drink

Brazilian Cuisine

Brazilian cuisine is fresh and exotic. With a colonial past, it is no wonder that the flavours are a blend of Portuguese and African influence. Brazilians have altered traditional dishes from these two backgrounds with local ingredients creating new flavours. Rio's dining etiquette does not specify when one should or shouldn't eat certain foods or where. Many of the traditional foods can easily be found in street markets (feiras), small cafés (botecos), restaurants and street vendors. Salgados are the Brazilian equivalent to fast food and are enjoyed throughout the day.

Caipirinhas

The national cocktail of Brazil can be easily found whether you're strolling along a beach or sitting inside a café. The Caipirinha (pronounced Kai-Pee-Reen-Ya) is an alcoholic beverage made from Cachaça (a sugar cane spirit), sugar and lime wedges. A summer time drink perfect the hot Brazilian climate. The sweet, fruity taste is easily paired with foods at any time of the day. The cost is fairly low depending on where you choose to purchase the drink. Variations of this drink include less sugar or different spirits other than Cachaça.

Coconut Water

Another beverage you will see a lot of people drinking in Brazil is coconut water straight from the coconut. With coconut trees on every street, it's not surprising they are a staple at the beach. Cool and refreshing, coconut water has exploded as a health beverage over the past few years. Options for ordering are in the glass or in the coconut itself. Due to sanitary concerns, most people recommend the coconut instead of a glass. Drinking from the coconut is really great photo opportunity!

Craft Beer

Craft brewing is a trend that is exploding throughout the world and Brazil is no exception. The majority of alcohol drunk in Brazil is beer. With a lot of small breweries to choose from, beer lovers can find a favourite in Rio to suit their palate. Due to high taxes, craft breweries are not that common in Rio, but there are a number to be found. Many local botecos or pubs carry craft beers. The beers range from pale ales to stouts; ensuring there is something to satisfy every beer aficionado.

Feijoada

This Brazilian stew pays homage to the country's Portuguese heritage and is made primarily with black beans and beef and/or pork. Seasoned with onions, garlic, bay leaves, thyme, paprika, pepper and vinegar. The stew is typically made with all parts of the animal including ears, tails and feet. Served with rice, farofa, cabbage and garnished with orange slices it is a national dish that has a lot of flavour. Enjoyed either for lunch or supper, it will give you the energy you need to explore this cultural city.

Farofa

This typical side dish to many Brazilian meat entrees like feijoada or barbequed meats, farofa is made from flour with onion, oil (usually palm), butter and seasoned with salt and pepper. Toasted in a skillet, it is similar in texture to tapioca. You can try it with eggs, bacon, olives, bananas and other add-ons depending on the vendor. While it can be eaten on its own, it is usually mixed in with other foods. A staple to many meals, farofa is not to be skipped.

Brazilian crepes

Served by street vendors and in restaurants alike, the Brazilian tapioca-flour crepes are different from French crepes. The tapioca crepes are filled with a variety of savory foods like cheese, vegetables, chocolate or a more-hearty beef filling. Made simply with cassava flour and water, these crepes are great for anyone who has a gluten allergy. Depending on the filling, these can be suitable for any diet. Although they are not overly flavourful in themselves, they are a great local food to try and can be enjoyed anytime of the day.

Moqueca

In a coastal city like Rio, you have to try the seafood dishes! A seafood stew made with salt water fish, prawns, coconut milk and spices Moqueca originates from the Bahia region in Brazil. Spiced with coriander, paprika, chili flakes, tomato, onion, red pepper, and a hint of garlic and lime juice the coconut milk gives the stew a creamy texture. It's this rich cream-based orange-tinted sauce that makes this dish a decadent treat. Eaten during mid-day or in the evening.

Churrascaria

Meat on swords makes for an exciting adventure in local cuisine! These are buffet style restaurants found throughout Rio. Waiters brings swords of meat to your table where they slice of pieces for you to enjoy. Simply say yes or no to the type of meat once it comes to your table; some places provide you with green and red cards to easily show the waiter what you want or don't want. It's all you can eat so feel free to explore different meats and cuts. Churrascaria, a Brazilian barbeque buffet is a must do on a trip to Rio.

Empadinahas

A dish that highlights the Portuguese connection, empadinahas are similar to empanadas in other parts of Latin America. These mini pies stuffed with a variety of fillings including savory meats, shrimp, chicken, corn, cheese or hearts of palm. Typically fried, it is possible to find baked versions. A hot pepper sauce can also be added for more spice. These mini pies can be found on the streets on in cafés. Eaten by itself as a snack or pair it with a side salad for a nice easy, quick meal.

Pastel

Essentially a Brazilian turnover, the pastel (pah-steh-oo) is a pastry filled with cheese, shrimp or beef. Step out of the normal and try one of the fancier versions like brie and apricot, or a dessert version featuring chocolate and bananas. These are half moon or rectangular in shape that can be deep-fried or baked depending on your preference. Easily found being sold by street vendors, restaurants and beach vendors. It is common for cariocas, the people of Rio, share these in cafés, bars and pubs.

Bolinho de Bacalhau

Drawing upon the Portuguese cuisine, the bolinho de bacalhau are salted cod fish cakes that are deep fried and served as an appetizer or a shared snack at a bar. Made with shredded dried and salted cod, potatoes, onion, egg, bay leaf, peppercorns and parsley they are typically served with a slice of lime. Well prepared bolinho de bacalhau should be crispy on the outside with a soft and slightly creamy filling. A chilli sauce or mayonnaise based dipping sauce may accompany the cakes.

Fruit

A tropical climate, visitors and residents of Rio have a wide variety of fruit to choose from on a daily basis. Bananas, banana-maça (apple flavoured bananas), cajú (cashew fruit), maracujá doce (sweet passion fruit) and mangoes are just some of the fruits that can be found throughout Rio. Açai is a very popular fruit that is in demand for its high antioxidants is grown locally and can be found cheaply. The street markets and vendors sell fruit throughout Rio.

Cheese bread

Pão de queijo in Portuguese, cheese bread is a popular snack that is both cheesy and crunchy. A ball shaped morsel, they can be easily found in bakeries, restaurants and on the streets. With a dense, slightly chewy inside, they can be quite filling. Not to be confused with cheese balls (bolinha de queijo) which are a doughy exterior with a melted cheese center. An on-the-go style snack, cheese bread is a must eat on a trip to Rio.

Coxinhas

Easily identified by their tear-drop shape, Coxinhas are a salgado that is filled with a creamy-cheese and chicken mixture encased in a whole wheat flour and potato dough. Deep-fried or baked, this tasty snack can be dipped in a spicy sauce. Depending on the vendor, you can get a coxinhas with a symbolic chicken bone (usually a toothpick) in the center, so be cautious on your first bite. One of the most popular salgados to be found and tried.

Acarajé

Originating from the north-eastern part of Brazil in Bahia acarajé is an example of the influence from African cuisine on Brazilian foods. This salgado is a deep-fried patty made up of crushed black-eyed peas and palm oil. The patties are cut open and typically stuffed with dried shrimp and a spicy paste called vatapá. Acarajé is a must try for any seafood lover. Add-ons to the basic version of this snack include coconut, cashews, garlic and more. Sold in markets the women, baianas, are easily recognizable in their costumes of all white.

Brigaderio

Small decadent chocolate balls similar to truffles, Brigaderio is a staple consumed at celebrations like birthday parties. The lore that surrounds the name of the treat is that Brigadier Eduardo Gomes wife gave these to supporters at his political campaign rallies to raise funds. There is a question as to whether it was his wife or just admirers. Despite the history of the name, this sweet treat is a national favourite. Made from condensed milk, powdered chocolate and butter rolled into balls, baked and then covered in sprinkles they can be found in bakeries, markets, restaurants and street vendors.

TO VISIT

Unusual cafés and bars

Rio has great cafés and bars spread out through its various neighbourhoods. The cafés and botecos (or pubs) are a great place to relax and enjoy a drink and some food. The bars and nightclubs are lively and full of music and samba. If you are going to a nightclub they use a consumption card which tracks how many drinks you have. You will need to show this and settle your bill before you leave.

Café du Lage

Quickly becoming a well-known haunt of celebrities and artists, this café is located inside the Parque Lage building which has been converted into an art institute (Escola de Artes Visuais do Parque Lage) at the bottom of Corcovado. Overlooking a scenic pool with majestic views in the background and offering food and beverage at a price lower than the cafés at the summit. The Café du Lage is the perfect spot to relax and recharge before or after a trip up Corcovado.

- R. Jardim Botânico, 414, Jardim Botânico, Rio de Janeiro, 22461-000 +55 21 2226 8125

Armazém São Thiago

A trendy restaurant and bar in Santa Teresa neighbourhood it is located in an old warehouse that dates back to 1917. What was once a corner grocer's shop is now a bar but maintains its original look and feel. Known by the locals as "Bar do Gomez," this bar brings the history of Rio and wonderful hospitality to a perfect junction. The drinks are cool and tasty and the food delicious. If you want to go where the locals go, then this is the spot.

- Rua Aurea 26, Santa Teresa, Rio de Janeiro, 20240-210 +55 21 2232-0822

Bip-Bip

A small, non-descript bar located on a backstreet in Copacabana, Bip-Bip features traditional bossa nova, samba de roda and choro music. The music rules the bar and patrons are respectful of the musicians who grace the stage. Musicians who perform here range from professionals to amateurs. Performed almost every night by live musicians to crowds of appreciative locals who are comfortable with standing room only. This is a place to visit if you're looking to listen to music.

- «Bip-Bip», Loja D, R. Alm. Gonçales, 50-Copacabana, Rio de Janeiro

Circo Voador

A popular venue if you're looking for national and international music to dance to in Rio, Circo Voador is in the Lapa district. Committed to supporting up and coming artists, the venue always has something interesting going on. While the music genres do vary from metal to samba, rock is the primary genre. If you like Brazilian Rock this is the venue to visit. Two floors of music and fairly low entry rates make this an affordable place. Rates for shows vary.

- Circo Voador, Rue do Arcos s/n 20230-060, Rio de Janeiro, Brazil, +55 21 2533 0354

Brewteco Leblon

A pub in Leblon offering craft beers from around Brazil. The boteco first opened in 1966, but has changed since then. It serves tasty pastels and pub food to snack on as well as beer. This is the perfect location for anyone who loves craft beer and wants to try what Brazil has to offer. The price of beer is more expensive than the standard beer you will find, with the cheapest starting around R$9.

- Rua Dias Ferreira, 420 – Ioja E- Leblon, Rio de Janeiro, 22431-050 +55 21 2512-3114

Café Severino

For booklovers everywhere, the Café Severino is a must for a coffee and sweet treat. Located inside Argumento, a bookshop, this café serves a variety of traditional pastries, sandwiches and snacks. Opened in 1996 the setting provides a nice quiet retreat from the buzz of the city. The prices here are slightly higher with entradas ranging from R$12 to R$36. Located in Leblon it's not surprising that the prices are higher, but worth a visit.

- Rua Dias Ferreira, 417, Leblon, Rio de Janeiro, 22431-050 +55 21 2259-9398

Rio Scenarium

Three floors of music at this popular venue are adorned with antiques and chandeliers. Located in a colonial mansion the Rio Scenarium is a great place for listening to music and dancing samba all night. There are three main rooms with different music playing in each room. Cover charge is about R$20-35. There is a restaurant on site that can be reserved in advance and the average price for an entrée is about R$50. Drinks and food can also be purchased in the bar area.

- Rio Scenarium, R. do Lauradio, 20-Centro, Rio de Janeiro, Brazil, +55 21 3147 9000

Bar Urca

A small, quaint little bar that is unassuming it has cold beer and tasty snacks. Entrees can get up to R$60 but most snacks are between R$5 and R$6.50. Grab your drink and snack and walk across the road to enjoy the bar's location and sit on the promenade overlooking the water. Sunset can see the railing get pretty busy as it's a popular after-work watering hole. There is a restaurant on the second level if you desire more of a sit-down meal.

- Bar Urca, Rua Cândido Gaffrée, 205, Urca, Rio de Janeiro, Brazil, +55 21 2295 8744

Bar Bukowski

Rio's most famous rock bar is located in Botafogo. Named for the famed American writer Charles Bukowski, Bar Bukowski is located in a colonial mansion and has two floors of rock music ranging from the Beatles to Amy Winehouse to Linkin Park and the Foo Fighters. Downstairs has a dance floor and upstairs has a live music venue. An outdoor courtyard and bar provide an alternate area for enjoying the atmosphere. Live shows and performances are a staple at this venue. Open only on Fridays, Saturdays and holidays entry is R$55.

- Rua Alvaro Ramos, 270, Rio de Janeiro, 22280-110 +55 21 2244-7303

Crazy Cats Bistro

A gastropub in the Botafogo district, Crazy Cats Bistro is a place to visit for an eclectic experience. If you like live music, jazz and rock, and a vintage vibe this is the perfect spot. They have tribute bands playing the Beatles, jazz and blues bands, 80s rock tribute bands and more. They always have something going on. With great service, good food and moderate prices for both the food and the drinks, which have fun names like Jagger, Crazy Cats is a must visit on a trip to Rio.

- Rua Sorocaba, 19 – Botofogo, Rio de Janeiro, 22271-110 +55 21 99106-9336

TO VISIT

Not tourist locations

Sitio Roberto Brule Marx

Located in the West Zone of Rio, the former home of renowned Brazilian artist Roberto Brule Marx is a sprawling property that includes his botanical and landscaped gardens and a museum. With over 3,500 plant species spanning 40 acres and climbing 400 meters in elevation, the property has a diverse landscape. This museum houses more than 3000 items, and the largest collection of his work. Marx lived on the property until he died in 1994. Tours are held daily by appointment only and cost R$10.

- Estrada de Guaratiba, 2019, Rio de Janeiro, 23020-240

Gávea

Gávea, located in the South Zone, is home to some of Rio's best educational institutions and as such has a unique feel. Here you will find the Instituto Moreira Salles, Rio's planetarium, the Jockey Club racetrack, a shopping mall and lots of hip cafés and bars. Located inside the shopping mall you will find a cinema that plays both Brazilian and international movies, and the Teatro das Artes. The botanical gardens and municipal park, Pedra dâ Gávea, are both located within a short walk.

Instituto Moreira Salles

Originally the home of Walther Moreira Salles, the Instituto is a cultural center of modern Rio. Located in Gávea, the institute showcases exhibits by new artists and has various collections including photography and literary. With film screenings, concerts and more, the Instituto is a hub of cultural activity. There is also a bookshop and restaurant. Admission is free to the house and exhibitions, but there is a fee for the cinema and special events. Open Tuesday-Sunday from 11am to 8pm.

- Rua Marques de Sao Vincente, 476, Gávea, Rio de Janeiro, 22451-044

Aquário Marinho do Rio

The largest aquarium in South America opened in 2016 and houses over 350 different species of marine life from ecosystems around the world. Spanning 26,000 m² with 28 tanks and holding 4.5 million litres of saltwater the Aquario Marinho do Rio has a R$100 entrance fee. In addition to a touch pool, visitors can swim with fish, rays and sharks, or walk through an undersea tunnel in the largest tank. Open daily from 10am-5pm.

- Via Binario do Porto, 194, Praca Muhammad Ali, Rio de Janeiro, 20220-360

Neimeyer's Museum of Contemporary Art

Located across the bay from Rio in Niterói, the Museum of Contemporary Art, known locally as the MAC looks out onto Guanabara Bay. It is one of many buildings in Rio designed by the famed Brazilian architect, Oscar Niemeyer. Opened in 1996, the exterior is a saucer shape with the interior housing a grand collection of contemporary art. It offers panoramic views of Rio. Open Tuesday-Sunday 10am-6pm, admission is R$10.

- Mirante da Boa Viagem, Niteroi, Rio de Janeiro, 24210-470

Governor's Island

Dating back to colonial times, Governor's Island sits in Guanabara Bay and is connected to the mainland by a bridge. Named Governor's Island or Ilha do governador in the 16th century after Governor of Brazil built a house there. It is now home to Rio's Galeão-Antônio Carlos Jobim International Airport and Galeão Air Force Base. The non-touristy area is home to a favela. It has a small restaurant scene and quiet neighbourhoods compared to the bustle of downtown Rio.

Museu Nacional de Belas Artes

Located in Centro, the Fine Arts Museum of Rio has over 20,000 pieces in its collection. Pieces displayed include sculptures and paintings from Brazil, Europe and Africa. The museum covers 18,000m² and has both permanent and temporary exhibitions. Officially created by Presidential decree in 1937 this is an important cultural center. While the building was opened in 1937, the collection dates back to 1808 when the Portuguese court moved to Brazil. Admission is free, but special exhibits may have a cost. Open Tuesday-Friday 10am-5pm, Saturday-Sunday 10am-1pm and closed Mondays.

- Av. Rio Branco, 199, Centro, Rio de Janeiro, 20040-008

Royal Portuguese Reading Room

Located in the Centro district of Rio, the Real Gabinete Portugues Da Leitura houses the largest collection of Portuguese literature outside of Portugal. Opened in 1887, the Gothic-Renaissance style reading room is well photographed and recognized as one of the most beautiful libraries in the world. Over 350,000 book line the walls, three stories high. The bookshelves draw your eye up to the ornate skylight and chandelier; the reading room is breathtaking. Admission is free. Open Monday-Friday 9am-6pm.

- Rua Luis de Camoes, 30, Centro, Rio de Janeiro, 20051-020

Municipal Theatre

An opulent cultural centre of Rio, the Teatro Municipal is in the Centro district. Frequently compared to the Opera in Paris, the building hosts performances by both national and international artists. The opulence of the façade continues to the interior of the building which is simply luxurious. Ballets, operas, symphony orchestras and concerts are held throughout the year. Re-opened in 2010 after two years of renovations, the 110year old building offers guided tours at the cost of R$10. Tours are held at specific times throughout the week.

- Praca Floriano, Rio de Janeiro, 20031-050

Sambódromo

The site of the internationally renowned Samba Parade that happens during Carnaval, the Sambódromo opened in 1984. Built specifically for the parade, it was designed by Oscar Niemeyer. At 700 meters in length it has a capacity of 90,000. The venue was renovated in time for the 2016 Olympics to improve the views of spectators. Seats range in price from the grandstands starting at $34US to the most expensive luxury seats at $1654US. Outside of carnival time, the area is used for concerts.

- Rua Marques de Sapucai, Rio de Janeiro, 22640-100

Centro Cultural Banco do Brasil Rio

One of three cultural centers in the country, the Centro Cultural Banco do Brasil in Rio opened in 1989 in a renovated art deco building in the Centro district. Said to be home to some of the best exhibitions in Brazil, the location has two theatres, a cinema, art galleries, restaurant, bookshop, coffeeshop and tea salon. A veritable hub of cultural events, you can frequently see lunchtime and evening concerts. Admission depends on the exhibit or event, but some are free. Open Wednesday-Monday from 9am-9pm.

- Rua Primeiro de Marco 66, Rio de Janeiro, 20010-000

Shopping in Leblon

If you want to experience something different, visit either Shopping Leblon or the Rio Design Mall. These malls are more than just shopping malls with libraries, exhibitions, cinemas, cafés and restaurants; they are an experience. Both have very active social media presence. If it is shopping you're interested in they do not disappoint. If you have mid-to high-end stores in mind including Hugo Boss, Chanel and Zara, Shopping Leblon is your place. For more local designers visit the Rio Design Mall.

- Shopping Leblon: Av. Afrânio de Melo Franco, 290 Leblon, Rio de Janeiro, 22430-060 +55 21 2430-5122
- Rio Design Mall: Avenida Ataulfo de Paiva 270, Rio de Janeiro, 22440-900 +55 21 3206-9110

Museu da Chácara do Céu

Once the home to a Brazilian businessman, Castro Maya, the Museu da Chácara do Céu houses his art collection. A modernist style building with a garden and overlooking Rio and Guanabara Bay. Some of the collection includes pieces by Dali, Degas, Matisse, Monet and Picasso. Also houses art by Brazilian artists and provides a perspective on the history of Brazil. Not overly crowded, this is a true hidden gem if you are a lover of art or architecture. Admission is R$6 for adults and R$3 for children. Open daily from 12pm-5pm, except Tuesdays.

- Rue Murtinho Nobre, 93, Santa Teresa, Rio de Janeiro, 20241-050

Sao Joao Batista Cemetary

Found in Botafogo the Sao Joao Batista Cemetery is reminiscent of Pére Lachaise in Paris. A massive burial ground with tombs from various architectural periods, the cemetery is the only one in southern part of Rio. Opened in 1852, this cemetery is the burial place for many of Brazils famous politicians and entertainers. Wandering through the labyrinth of tombs can take the majority of your time. Save some for exploring the lesser known parts like the anjinhos (little angels) which is the secluded burial spot up the hill of the poorest children. Incredibly moving and interesting, the cemetery is open daily at 7am-5pm.

- Rua General Polidoro, Botafogo, Rio de Janeiro

Feira de Arte de Ipanema

Started in the 1960s the Feira de Arte de Ipanema, or Hippie Market in Ipanema now has over 700 stalls. Stalls offer a variety of items from cheap souvenirs to hand made art and crafts including leather sandals, wooden boxes, ceramics, paintings and more. Open on Sundays only from 10am-5pm, this is one trip that needs to be planned. The outdoor market this is the perfect place to spend a Sunday wandering, shopping for some unique souvenirs and eating some delicious authentic food. The market is open rain or shine.

- Rua Visconde de Piraia, Praca General Osorio, Rio de Janeiro, 22410-020

TO VISIT   *Top 5 Beaches*

A trip to Rio would not be complete without visiting some of its most famous scenery, the beach. You don't have to be an avid beach goer to enjoy the charm of the beaches and scenery offered. Elaborate sandcastles are created by locals for people to see. For those who want to go on foot, you can walk from Copacabana to Leblon via the beach and promenade. It takes about an hour and a half but is an easy, fairly flat walk.

Copacabana Beach

One of the most well-known beaches in the world, Copacabana is located on the Atlantic Ocean. Local bands play at bars near the beaches to entice customers to sit and sip while watching a magnificent sunset. Three miles long, this beach becomes very busy throughout the day. Perhaps the best time to enjoy may be during the morning. During the day you can rent bicycles and pedal along the sandy beach giving you a different view.

Red Beach

Located in the district of Urca and across the square from where the cable car ascends to the top of Sugarloaf, the Red Beach sits on Guanabara Bay. Known locally as Praia Vermelha, this beach is less crowded than the popular tourist beaches and provides stunning views. Looming over the beach is Sugarloaf Mountain. Although not the best for swimming due to pollution levels in the Bay, the scenery is unparalleled, especially at sunset when the beach is blanketed in hues of red, giving it the name Red Beach.

Ipanema Beach

Popular for swimming, beach volleyball and relaxing on a beach chair with coconut water or a caipirinha, Ipanema provides views of the ocean with a mountain in the distance. Located in what is considered to be one of the most well-to-do areas of Rio, Ipanema beach is just steps from high end shopping. Chances are you will likely see some of the most beautiful people in Brazil at this beach which is where people come to be seen. Three kilometer stretch of beach, fresh fruit stands are abundant here and make healthy snacking easy.

Leblon Beach

Located just across a small canal from Ipanema, Leblon gives visitors a less busy beach experience. The feel of the Leblon area extends to the beach with its more bohemian vibe. More families tend to visit this beach compared to its neighbour Ipanema. In the evenings the beach has several sports being played including beach volleyball, foot volley ball and football (soccer). There are trendy bars and restaurants just steps away from the beach which makes for great eating and drinking.

Prainha Beach

A short drive from Rio's downtown to the west, you will find more beaches. A beach that is near perfect to visit is Piranha, about a 45- minute drive. A vehicle is required to reach this beach which has the added benefit of it being nearly empty during the weekdays. It is also flanked by two rocky cliffs which make for some great surfing opportunities. Add the lush rainforest vegetation that hugs the beach and you have your picture postcard ready scene.

TO VISIT

Outdoor adventures and nature

Rio is a city that calls for outdoor adventures. The climate and natural landscape provide numerous activities for visitors and locals alike. From heart-stopping mountain trekking and hang gliding to strolling along a beach or wandering through a garden there is something for everyone.

Sugarloaf

Pão de Acucar is often confused with Corcovado with many tourists expecting to see Christ the Redeemer at the top. Located in Urca, Sugarloaf is an impressive 396 meters high. To reach the summit you take a cable car which provides impressive views of Rio. It is a two-stage cable car. One car takes riders from the base in Urca to the first top of Morro da Urca and the second goes to the top of Sugarloaf. Offering panoramic views of the city, it is an ideal spot to watch the sun dip below the horizon. Open Sunday-Saturday 8am-7:45pm.

- Av. Pasteur, 520, Rio de Janeiro, 22290-255

Botanical Gardens

The Jardim Botânico founded in 1808 and opened to the public in 1822 is home to 6,000 types of plants and trees. This internationally recognized garden stretches over 330 acres. Taking a few hours or a day to stroll its many walking paths and explore its fountains, sculptures, monuments and more is a great way to see the diversity and richness of the rainforest. A café provides a nice spot for 6pm.

- Rua Jardim Botanico, 1008, Jardim Botânico, Rio de Janeiro, 22470-180

Selarón Stairway

A colourful artistic restoration of a set of stairs in Rio's Lapa neighbourhood, the Escadaria Selarón is a must-see location. Chilean born artist, Jorge Selarón, began working on the steps in 1990 and continued until his death in 2013. The stairway has over 215 steps covered in tiles from around the world. The bright, vibrant colours are the artist's "tribute to the Brazilian people." At 125 meters high the stairway connects the areas of Lapa and Santa Teresa. A lot of street art can also be seen around the stairway giving insight into life in Rio.

- Rua Joaquim Silva, Rio de Janeiro, 20241-110

Recreios do Bandeirantes

Located on the western edge of Rio, Recrios dos Bandeirantes is the name of both a beach and neighbourhood. Containing jungles, rocky cliffs and a beautiful stretch of beach, the area offers a lot for outdoor activities. The beach offers surfing and beach volleyball with the added bonus of being less busy than the iconic Copacabana or Ipanema beaches. It also has a boardwalk for strolling down and enjoying a beverage and a snack.

Lagoa Rodrigo de Freitas

In the South Zone of Rio, the Lagoa Rodrigro de Freitas is a beautiful spot for exploring the natural beauty of Rio. Connected to the Atlantic Ocean, this saltwater lagoon has nearly one square mile of surface. The lagoon has walking trails and a paved 7km bike path. Bikes can be easily rented and for those who would prefer to go across rather than around, paddle boats can be used. Food vendors can be found around the lagoon providing refreshments to people enjoying the outdoors.

- Av. Epitacio Pessoa, Rio de Janeiro, 22471-001

Favela tour

The favelas are the controversial slums of Brazil. Created when people just started building and living illegally on lands in the city, they are home to some of the most dangerous areas. Prior to the Olympics in 2016 they were heavily raided by police. Since then, tours of the areas have become popular. It is recommended that you go with a tour rather than explore individually. Tours highlight the daily struggles of the residents and considering one third of Rios population live in the favelas, they can provide insight into these developments.

Quinta da Boa Vista

Located in the north zone of Rio, the Quinta da Boa Vista is a city park that encompasses the gardens and palace of the São Cristóvão Palace. The gardens are an example of English-style landscaping with sweeping lawns and tall trees. Covering 155 m² they are free to visit. The park it well used by cariocas who picnic here regularly. Originally home to the Emperors of Brazil and most recently the National Museum, the palace itself burned down in September 2018.

- Av. Pedro II, Sao Cristovao, Rio de Janeiro, 20941-070

Pedra do Sal

The birthplace of Samba, the Pedra do Sal or Rock of Salt is a small plaza in the neighbourhood of Saúde. Located west of the downtown, it is the home of the descendants of African slaves from the Bahia region in northern Brazil. The area is a culturally significant place for many African religions. Samba was born here and is practiced weekly with sessions held every Monday evening, weather permitting. Access to the plaza is free and you can join in the dancing easily.

- Largo Joao da Baiana, Sáude, Rio de Janeiro, 20081-120

Paquetá Island

Located in Guanabara Bay, Paquetá Island is a car free zone. A peaceful oasis just one hour from the hustle and bustle of Rio. While crowded on weekends, the island has colonial style/era buildings that exude a quaint charm and restaurants that cater to the palate. One of the more unique aspects of the island is a bird cemetery for the burial of beloved pet fowl. Although the beaches are not the best, the scenery and peacefulness make this island a worthy trip.

Santa Teresa Tram

The oldest and first electric tram in Latin America, the Santa Teresa Tram is still running. Although it has not run consistently and is only partially operational, it is still worth a visit. The rustic cars are a distinctive yellow and riding the tram gives you a feeling of being transported back in time. The open sided carriage provides a different view of the streets of the hilltop Santa Teresa. The tram runs Monday-Friday 8am-5:30pm, Saturday 10am-5pm and Sunday 11am-4:30pm. Cost is R$20.

- Rua Lelio Gama, 2, Rio de Janeiro, 20031-080

Parque Nacional da Tijuca

Located in the heart of Rio, the 120km² rainforest of Tijuca Park is a contrast to the development of the sprawling modern-day Rio. Tijuca holds the title as the world's largest urban forest. With more than 150 trails to traverse this is truly the jungle in the city. Along the trails you can find waterfalls like the famed Cascatinha Waterfall, picnic areas and caves. You can visit the park on your own or with a tour group which is recommended if you want to take a less travelled trail.

- Estrada da Cascatinha, 850, Alto da Boa Vista, Rio de Janeiro, 20531-590

Rock Climbing in Rio

With many large mountains and steep cliffs and amazing sceneries of ocean and forest, Rio is a rock climbers paradise. There are many options for the experienced climber including the famed Corcovado and Sugarloaf mountains. If you're not an experienced rock climber and would like to take try Rio offers a multitude of locations to learn. You can take a one-day classes or tours with experienced guides who will show you the ropes. Guides are recommended for many of the ascents.

Pista Cláudio Coutinho

A two-kilometer trail just off the Red Beach in Urca, the Pista Cláudio Coutinho gives inexperienced hikers the opportunity to enjoy some of the tropical forest by foot. An easy hike, the trail exposes visitors to some of the lush flora and fauna of the Tijuca Forest. You enter the trail via the parking lot on the left side of the Red Beach. If you are interested, you can take the trail up to Morro da Urca which is the first stage of the cable car ascent to Sugarloaf Mountain. Open daily from 6am to 6pm.

Arpoador

Located in Copacabana, Arpoador is known for its surf and surfers. Watching the surfers is a past-time. Waves can be found at almost any tide and can become crowded and aggressive. The currents can change easily and the number of surfers on the water usually indicates how strong the current is: fewer surfers means a stronger current. There are a lot of spectators at Arpoador. If watching the surfers makes you want to try your hand at surfing in Rio, other beaches might be a better fit.

Pedra dâ Gávea

A large granite mountain with a flat top, Pedra dâ Gávea is located in the Tijuca forest. Higher at its peak than Corcovado, this mountain provides a difficult challenge for hikers taking about 2-3 hours to reach the summit. The trails date back to the 1880s and are well maintained. The hike begins in the tropical rainforest and you ascend for two hours under the canopy. Its height and spectacular views make it a popular climb for adventure seekers. A quick way off the mountain is paragliding.

Dois Irmaos

If you're looking for a different view of Rio than those offered by the more popular Sugarloaf and Corcovado, Dois Irmaos is for you. You can see the three main beaches, Christ the Redeemer and the Lagoa Rodrigo de Freitas from the top. An added bonus is no fee when you get to the summit and fewer people crowding the top. While a fairly easy hike compared to Sugarloaf you need shoes with treads and the trail can be steep in parts.

Hang gliding at Pedra Bonita

A perfect place to cross hang-gliding off your bucket list! The Pedra Bonita is also located in the Tijuca Park. You take an easy climb to the top of Pedra Bonita which provides beautiful views of the city below. From here you soar down to the Sao Conrado Beach. If you don't feel like hang gliding, you can watch as others soar the skies to the beach below. There are several schools that offer lessons and prices begin around US$200. You can book directly with the schools or through tour agencies.

Parque Lage

A lovely park tucked in at the foot of Corcovado Mountain, Parque Lage is often overlooked. It's mansion that now houses the art school is gaining notice since Snoop Dogg made a video there, but the park itself still remains peaceful. The mansion dates back to the 1880s and was home to a Brazilian industrialist, Enrique Lage and his wife. The gardens pre-date the mansion having been designed in the 1840s by John Tyndale.

- Rua Jardim Botanico, 414, Rio de Janeiro, 22461-000

Ruins Park

A Municipal park located in Santa Teresa, close to the San Bento Monastery, the Municipal Parque das Ruínas is one that is not heavily frequented by tourists. Formerly the home of Laurinda Santos Lobo, a great patroness of the arts in the early 1900s, the mansion fell into disrepair in the late twentieth century. Renovated in 1994 by the government, the park has become a cultural center that celebrates the visual and performance arts among the ruins. Open from Tuesday to Sunday, 8am to 8pm with free admission.

- Rua Murtinho Nobre, 169, Rio de Janeiro, 20241-050

Samba lessons

In addition to Pedra do Sal, samba lessons can be found throughout Rio, especially in the months leading up to Carnaval. You can choose to take samba lessons from one of the many samba schools that are located around the Sambódromo or you can choose to learn in the many local bars that play samba music. Locals are usually very happy to help you learn the steps. Also, the months leading up to Carnaval are full of opportunities to learn samba. Many of the schools get ready with rehearsal parties that are held each week. Just choose your favourite school.

TO STAY

Cool and unusual hostels

When it comes to staying in Rio, hostels can be the best bet to help save money and meet fellow explorers. Hostels can be found all over Rio, it depends on what is of most interest to you. You can choose to stay close to a beach, the nightlife, quiet neighbourhoods, favelas, the list goes on.

Rio Forest Hostel

Located in Santa Teresa, the Rio Forest Hostel lives up to its name with the forest encroaching on the hostel, or is it the hostel encroaching on the forest? You decide. This hostel offers both dorms and private rooms. Some of the benefits are a pool with a deck, bar, free breakfast, free wifi, air-conditioned guest rooms, guest kitchen, and friendly staff. Being in Santa Teresa gives the added bonus of beautiful views of the downtown and Bay area. Cost for accommodations start at around R$40.

- R. Joaquim Murtinho, 517 – Santa Teresa, Rio de Janeiro, 20241-320

Discovery Hostel

A boutique hostel located in Gloria, at the foot of Santa Teresa neighbourhood, it offers both shared and private rooms. This is a great spot for anyone looking to meet fellow travellers.

Many amenities are offered including free wifi, free breakfast, outdoor terrace, café and bar. Less than two miles from the downtown and close to the metro make it great for exploring. Price for rooms start around R$50.

- Rua Benjamin Constant, 26 – Glória, Rio de Janeiro, 20241-150

Chill Hostel

Located in a favela, this hostel offers a different experience for someone looking to explore Rio's more complex side. Transport delivers you to the bottom of the hill where you have to walk up to the hostel at the top. Very close to Copacabana beach the hostel has some impressive architecture having been designed by Oscar Niemeyer. Shared and private rooms are available. Offering free wifi, games room, communal kitchen and an outdoor terrace with views of Leme beach rooms begin at R$27.

- Ladeira Ary Barroso 35, Rio de Janeiro, 22010-060

Café Rio Hostel

Located in the Laranjeiras neighbourhood, bordering the Botafogo area, the Café Rio Hostel offers both shared and private rooms. The quiet neighbourhood offers restaurants, bars and shopping. The colourful walls and eclectic décor give a sense of warmth and comfort to this hostel. Friendly owners and staff add to the appeal of this small hostel. Amenities include free wifi, free breakfast, bar and air-conditioned bedrooms. Prices start around R$50.

- Rua Alice, 293, Laranjeiras, Rio de Janeiro

Tupiniquim Hostel

Authentic Brazilian experience is the best way to describe a stay at Tupiniquim hostel in Rio's Botafogo district. Offering only Brazilian cuisine to guests and promoting Brazilian music and movies this hostel helps you immerse yourself into the local culture. Free wifi, free breakfast, air conditioning and a rooftop terrace are some of the amenities offered. Both shared and private rooms are available. Shared dorms begin at around R$30.

- Rua Paulo Barreto, 79, Botafogo, Rio de Janeiro

Villa 25 Hostel

For a more boutique-style hostel experience try the Villa 25 in Flamengo. Boasting both a gastropub and a swimming pool, this trendy hostel feels anything but a hostel. Other amenities include free breakfast, free wifi, air conditioning, a steam room and an elevator. Easy access to the transportation and walking distance to Flamengo beach. Prices begin at approximately R$55 for a shared dorm.

- Rua Gago Coutinho, 25, Laranjeiras, Rio de Janeiro

Mambembe Hostel

Located in Santa Teresa district, just a five-minute walk from the heart of the Rio nightlife, this hostel is also a short walk to the beach. Offering shared and private accommodations, the Mambembe Hostel is ideal for travellers looking to stay close to the action. With a music room, sitting room, dining room and lots of outdoor space this hostel provides lots of opportunities to mingle with fellow guests. Prices begin around R$30.

- Rua Joaquim Murtinho, 251, Santa Teresa, Rio de Janeiro

Lemon Spirit Hostel

The Lemon Spirit Hostel has the status of being the first hostel in the Leblon district. Now into its tenth year, this hostel is located in an old heritage building that has been nicely renovated. Bright colours on the walls in some of the common areas, including a lovely lemony yellow gives a fun feel to the atmosphere at this place. Small but clean this hostel also offers free wifi, free breakfast and a bar. Shared rooms begin at around R$40.

- Rua Cupertino Durao, 56, Leblon, Rio de Janeiro

Green Culture Eco Hostel

This hostel is located in one of the first favelas that was pacified in 2009. A family like feel in a favela is waiting for you at this hostel thanks to the warm staff. Rooms are basic but clean. Offering free wifi, laundry facilities and a BBQ in a small village like setting just 10 minutes from Copacabana beach, the Green Culture Eco Hostel is ideal for anyone looking for an adventure and cultural experience. Shared rooms begin around R$55.

- Rua Dr. João Guerra – Chapeu Mangueira, Rio de Janeiro, 22010-060

Bonita Ipanema Pousada & Hostel

Located close to the Lagoon and the Hippie Market, the Bonita Ipanema hostel is the former home of Tom Jobim who wrote the song "Girl from Ipanema." A short distance from the beach, restaurants, pubs and transportation offers a great location for those seeking to explore Rio. A small pool, bar, games room, free wifi and free breakfast add to the charm of the historic building that is brightly painted. The shared dorms begin around R$60.

- Rua Barao da Torre, 107, Rio de Janeiro, 22411-001

TO BUY

Souvenirs

When traveling it can be overwhelming to decide what to buy and what not to buy to bring home as a souvenir. The following is a list that may help you narrow down you search for the perfect reminder of your time in Rio.

Art

Beautiful paintings and ceramics by talented local artists can be found in Rio. Bringing one home to add to your daily décor and serve as a daily reminder of a great trip. It can also be a conversational piece when you have guests over for caipirinhas during a Brazilian football match. Pieces can be found in high-end from the street markets is you are likely to be purchasing directly from the artist.

Jewellery

You can find lots of jewellery in Rio depending on your taste and budget. The prevalence of gemstones in Brazil makes fining jewellery featuring them fairly easy. For high-end jewellery check out some of the shops and malls in Leblon and Ipanema. If you are looking for less expensive jewellery, you can check out the wares of the beach vendors. These can be found for R$5. For more unique and handmade jewellery check out the stalls at the Hippie Market.

Sandals

Don't bother packing a pair of sandals for your trip to Rio. Instead, buy them when you get to Rio! Home to the world famous Havaianas or Ipanema flip flops, Brazil is the cheapest place to purchase these trendy sandals. Why not buy them in Brazil if you're going to be there anyway? You can find a wide variety of colours and designs to suit your personal preferences. Typically found ranging in price from R$10 to R$70 they can be found in shops around the beaches.

Hammock

Predating colonialism, the hammock was a traditional bed to keep you off the ground and minimize exposure to creepy critters. Now used for relaxation, the hammock is a comfortable, useful and unique souvenir to bring home from a trip to Brazil. Made from a variety of materials including canvas, cotton and rope that may have crocheted patterns, hammocks come in various styles and colours. Can range in price but budget for around R$100.

Brazilian coffee

Rio has many cafés and bistros where coffee is a staple. The coffee is still one of the most important economic exports for the country. Known for its flavour throughout the world, Brazilian coffee is a great souvenir to bring home. The type and cost of the coffee can vary widely. Purchasing a local brand in a small café may be better in taste and rich bold flavour than picking up a bag of one of the more popular brands at the supermarket. Enjoying a cup of strong coffee that invokes the memories of sitting in a café in Rio once you've returned home is a great way to remember your trip.

Cachaça

A spirit that is sweet, spicy and fruity in taste, Cachaça is made from sugar cane and used primarily in the creation of Caipirinhas. It is gaining popularity and people are including it in different cocktails. Like many spirits, they can range in price and quality. They can be purchased from a local supermarket. Some of the best brands include Beija, Milagre de Minas, Ypicoa, Minas Gerais, Germana and Magnifica. What a great way to continue to try different cocktails from Rio in your home?

Brazilian football team jersey

Football (or soccer in North America) is the national sport of Brazil. The yellow jersey is arguably one of the most widely recognized in the world. Why not take home a Brazilian football team jersey to wear during the next World Cup? When purchasing a jersey, you can save money by picking up one that is of less quality from street vendor. If you want an official jersey either for the quality or to support the team, your best bet is to purchase it from one of the licenced stores.

Caipirinha Kit

Bring a bit of your trip to Rio home with you. After a day of work or relaxing on the weekend in your hammock, wouldn't it be nice to reminisce about your fabulous trip to Rio over a caipirinha or two? A caipirinha kit can help make it easy instead of trying to recreate the drink from scratch. Average price for a caipirinha kit is R$30.

Wooden carvings

Sold at small markets and shops, handmade wooden carvings are a great souvenir to bring home. From iconic doves, to representations of Christ the Redeemer to wooden boxes, these souvenirs can be a lovely reminder of your trip. Made by local artisans the wooden boxes have inlaid wooden designs that can be pictorial or iconic. You can also find some that have agate, a natural geode from Brazil, inlaid in the top. Prices will vary.

Beachwear

Sarongs, bikinis and sungas are popular on the beaches in Brazil and a great souvenir. There are many places that sell them and range in a variety of quality and cost. You can choose your price point and style. Two of the best-known Brazilian brands are Blue Man and Farm. With the prevalence of the beach in daily life in Rio, you can find beachwear easily at any time of the year. Price for beachwear will vary from a low of R$5 up to over R$300 depending on your choice of vendor, brand and style.

Printed in Great Britain
by Amazon

43784289R00024